Herb Gardens
IN CROSS STITCH
Elena Thomas
D0413463
Anna
MEREHURST

In Memory of my Mum

THE CHARTS

Some of the designs in this book are very detailed and, due to inevitable space limitations, the charts may be shown on a comparatively small scale; in such cases, readers may find it helpful to have the particular chart with which they are currently working enlarged.

THREADS

The projects in this book were all stitched with DMC stranded cotton embroidery threads. The keys given with each chart also list thread combinations for those who wish to use Anchor or Madeira threads. It should be pointed out that the shades produced by different companies vary slightly, and it is not always possible to find identical colours in a different range.

Published in 1997 by Merehurst Limited
Ferry House, 51-57 Lacy Road, Putney, London SW15 1PR

ISBN 1 85391 531 9

A catalogue record for this book is available from the British Library.

Edited by Diana Lodge
Designed by Maggie Aldred
Photography by Juliet Piddington
Illustrations by John Hutchinson (pp5-7) and King & King (pp7, 14 and 39)
Typesetting by Dacorum Type & Print, Hemel Hempstead
Colour separation by CH Colourscan, Malaysia
Printed in Hong Kong by Wing King Tong

CONTENTS

INTRODUCTION

People have been growing herbs for thousands of years for both culinary and medicinal purposes. Now, by following the designs in this book, they can be used for decorative reasons too.

Some of the charts – for example, the ones for lavender and mint – are very simple. Others, such as the ones for the conservatory cushion and the bay tree hanging, are more complicated. Some of the designs can be customized for your own purposes.

The bay tree hanging includes a little beading, which is ideal for those keen cross stitchers who are looking to add an extra dimension to their work. If you are eager to experiment with less usual fabrics, the napkins are stitched with gold thread through waste canvas. All of the projects in this book are decorative, but some are also practical, functional items. I hope that the towel, napkins and cushions will be used with pleasure for many years after they have been stitched.

The project charts are accompanied by their own particular instructions, and in addition to this, the basic skills section gives general advice and help in preparing and completing your work.

Whether you pick up this book as a beginner or as a more experienced cross stitcher, able to adapt the designs for your own needs, I hope you find plenty to keep you interested and to keep your needle busy!

BASIC SKILLS

BEFORE YOU BEGIN

PREPARING THE FABRIC

Even with an average amount of handling, many evenweave fabrics tend to fray at the edges, so it is a good idea to overcast the raw edges, using ordinary sewing thread, before you begin.

FABRIC

Most of the projects in this book use Aida fabric, which is ideal for beginners and more advanced stitchers as it has a surface of clearly designated squares, each cross stitch being worked over a square. Other projects use 28-count evenweave fabric, which has 28 threads each way, embroidery stitches being taken over two threads.

If you wish to use a fabric with a different stitch count, count the maximum number of stitches on the chart horizontally and vertically and divide these numbers by the stitch count of your chosen fabric; this will give you the dimensions of the design when stitched on your fabric.

THE INSTRUCTIONS

Each project begins with a full list of the materials that you will require. The measurements given for the embroidery fabric include a minimum of 5cm (2in) all around to allow for stretching it in a frame and preparing the edges to prevent them from fraying.

Colour keys for stranded embroidery cottons – Anchor, DMC, or Madeira – are given with each chart. It is assumed that you will need to buy one skein of each colour mentioned in a particular key, even though you may use less, but where two or more skeins are needed, this information is included in the main list of requirements.

Before you begin to embroider, always mark the centre of the design with two lines of basting stitches, one vertical and one horizontal, running from edge to edge of the fabric, as indicated by the arrows on the charts.

As you stitch, use the centre lines given on the

chart and the basting threads on your fabric as reference points for counting the squares and threads to position your design accurately.

WORKING IN A HOOP

A hoop is the most popular frame for use with small areas of embroidery. It consists of two rings, one fitted inside the other; the outer ring usually has an adjustable screw attachment so that it can be tightened to hold the stretched fabric in place. Hoops are available in several sizes, ranging from 10cm (4in) in diameter to quilting hoops with a diameter of 38cm (15in). Hoops with table stands or floor stands attached are also available.

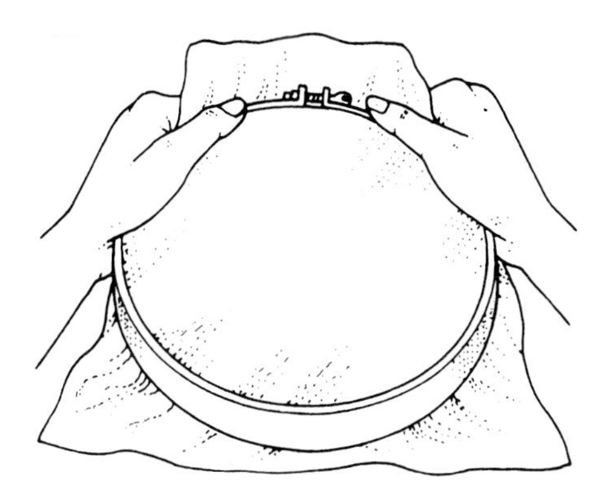

1 To stretch your fabric in a hoop, place the area to be embroidered over the inner ring and press the outer ring over it, with the tension screw released. Tissue paper can be placed between the outer ring and the embroidery, so that the hoop does not mark the fabric. Lay the tissue paper over the fabric when you set it in the hoop, then tear away the central embroidery area.

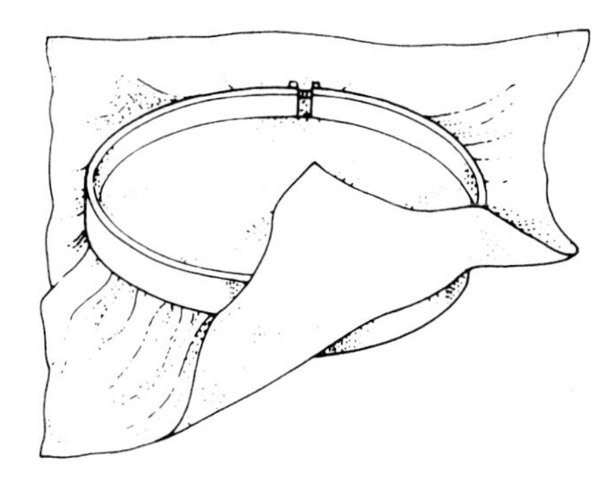

2 Smooth the fabric and, if necessary, straighten the grain before tightening the screw. The fabric should be evenly stretched.

WORKING IN A RECTANGULAR FRAME

Rectangular frames are more suitable for larger pieces of embroidery. They consist of two rollers, with tapes attached, and two flat side pieces, which slot into the rollers and are held in place by pegs or screw attachments. Available in different sizes, either alone or with adjustable table or floor stands, frames are measured by the length of the roller tape, and range in size from 30cm (12in) to 68cm (27in).

As alternatives to a slate frame, canvas stretchers and the backs of old picture frames can be used. Provided there is sufficient extra fabric around the finished size of the embroidery, the edges can be turned under and simply attached with drawing pins (thumb tacks) or staples.

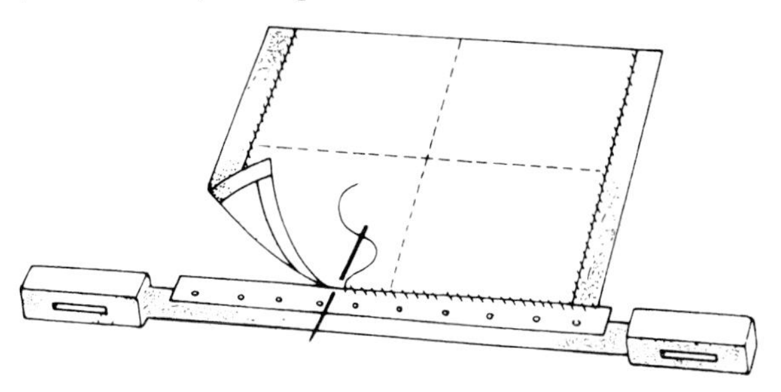

1 To stretch your fabric in a rectangular frame, cut out the fabric, allowing at least an extra 5cm (2in) all around the finished size of the embroidery. Baste a single 12mm (½in) turning on the top and bottom edges and oversew strong tape, 2.5cm (1in) wide, to the other two sides. Mark the centre line both ways with basting stitches. Working from the centre outward and using strong thread, oversew the top and bottom edges to the roller tapes. Fit the side pieces into the slots, and roll any extra fabric on one roller until the fabric is taut.

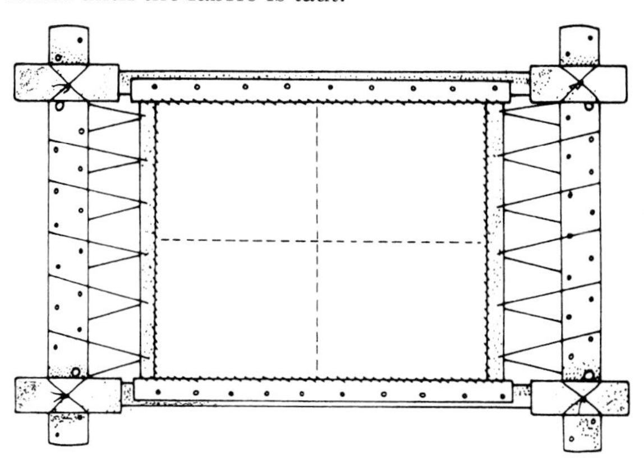

2 Insert the pegs or adjust the screw attachments to secure the frame. Thread a large-eyed needle (chenille needle) with strong thread or fine string and lace both edges, securing the ends around the intersections of the frame. Lace the webbing at 2.5cm (1in) intervals, stretching the fabric evenly.

EXTENDING EMBROIDERY FABRIC

It is easy to extend a piece of embroidery fabric, such as a bookmark, to stretch it in a hoop.

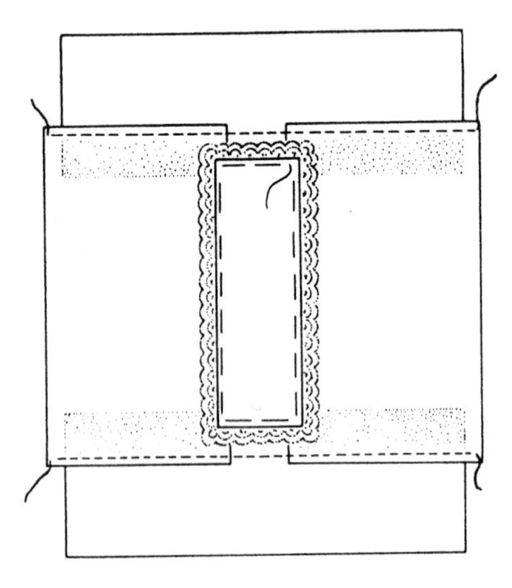

● Fabric oddments of a similar weight can be used. Simply cut four pieces to size (in other words, to the measurement that will fit both the embroidery fabric and your hoop) and baste them to each side of the embroidery fabric before stretching it in the hoop in the usual way.

THE STITCHES

CROSS STITCH

For all cross stitch embroidery, the following two methods of working are used. In each case, neat rows of vertical stitches are produced on the back of the fabric.

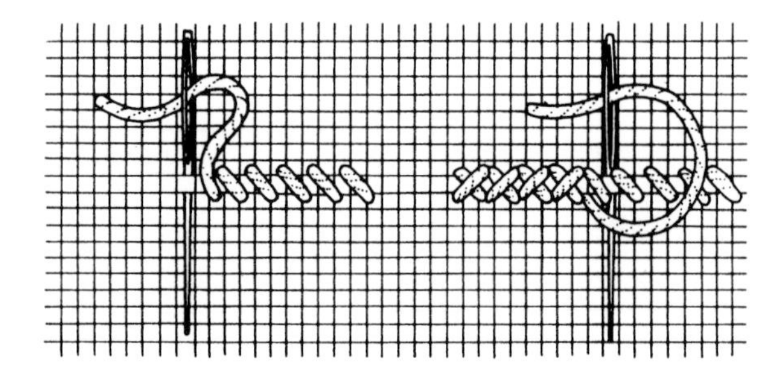

● When stitching large areas, work in horizontal rows. Working from right to left, complete the first row of evenly spaced diagonal stitches over the number of threads specified in the project instructions. Then, working from left to right, repeat the process. Continue in this way, making sure each stitch crosses in the same direction.

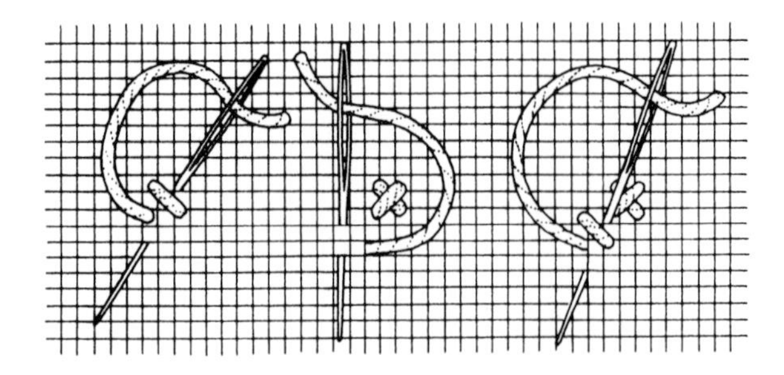

● When stitching diagonal lines, work downwards, completing each stitch before moving to the next. When starting a project always begin to embroider at the centre of the design and work outwards to ensure that the design will be placed centrally on the fabric.

BACKSTITCH

Backstitch is used in the projects to give emphasis to a particular foldline, an outline or a shadow. The stitches are worked over the same number of threads as the cross stitch, forming continuous straight or diagonal lines.

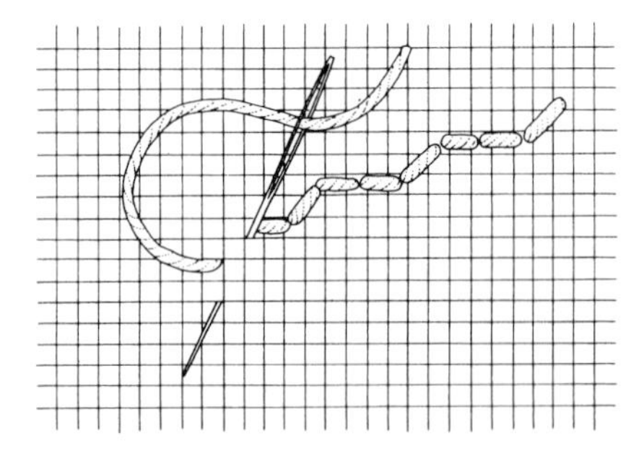

● Make the first stitch from left to right; pass the needle behind the fabric and bring it out one stitch length ahead to the left. Repeat and continue in this way along the line.

THREE-QUARTER CROSS STITCHES

Some fractional stitches are used on certain projects in this book; although they strike fear into the hearts of less experienced stitchers they are not difficult to master, and give a more natural line in certain instances. Should you find it difficult to pierce the centre of the Aida block, simply use a sharp needle to make a small hole in the centre

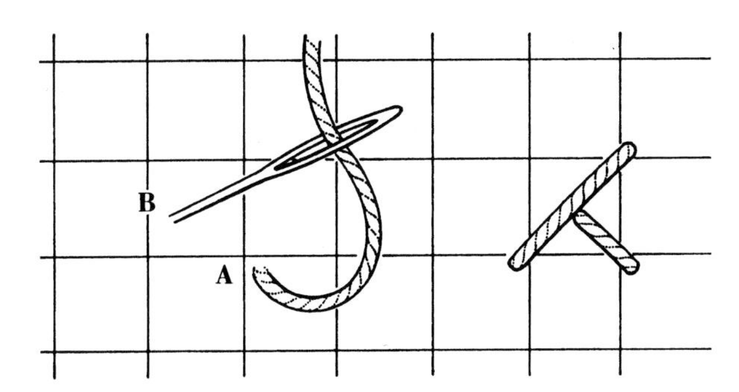

before making a stitch.

To work a three-quarter cross, bring the needle up at point A and down through the centre of the square at B. Later, the diagonal back stitch finishes the stitch. A chart square with two different symbols separated by a diagonal line requires two 'three-quarter' stitches. Backstitch will later finish the square.

BEADING

Any cross stitch chart can be used for beadwork instead of stitching. Each square on the chart represents one bead stitched onto an evenweave fabric, just as the crosses would be.

The small seed beads are stitched onto the fabric with a fine beading needle threaded with a matching colour. Use a diagonal stitch (half cross stitch) to attach the bead. Make sure all the stitches are worked in the same direction to ensure that the beads sit evenly on the fabric.

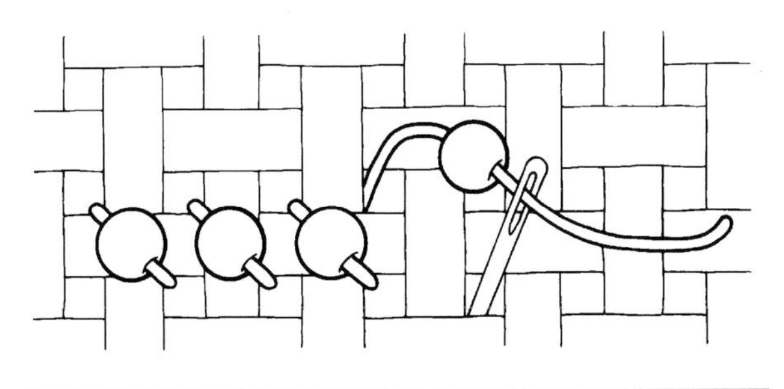

FINISHING

MOUNTING EMBROIDERY

The cardboard should be cut to the size of the finished embroidery, with an extra amount added all round to allow for the recess in the frame.

LIGHTWEIGHT FABRICS

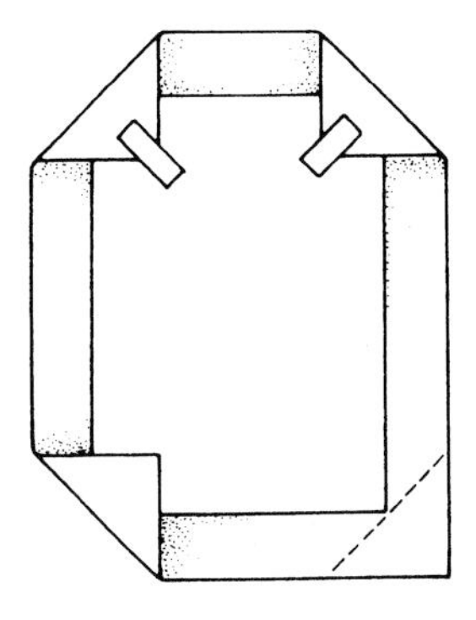

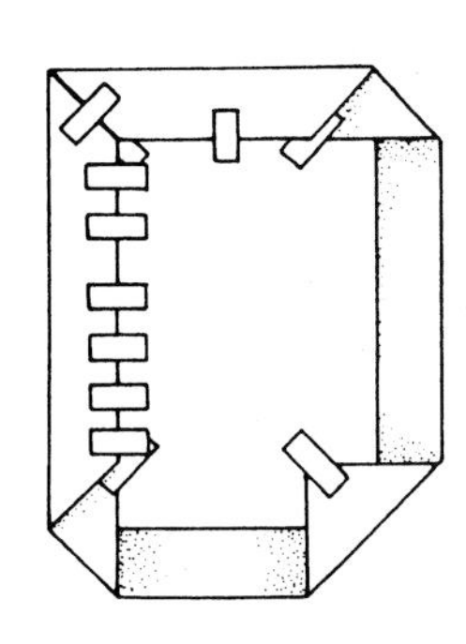

1 Place embroidery face down, with the cardboard centred on top, and basting and pencil lines matching. Begin by folding over the fabric at each corner and securing it with masking tape.

2 Working first on one side and then the other, fold over the fabric on all sides and secure it firmly with pieces of masking tape, placed about 2.5cm (1in) apart. Also neaten the mitred corners with masking tape, pulling the fabric tightly to give a firm, smooth finish.

HEAVIER FABRICS

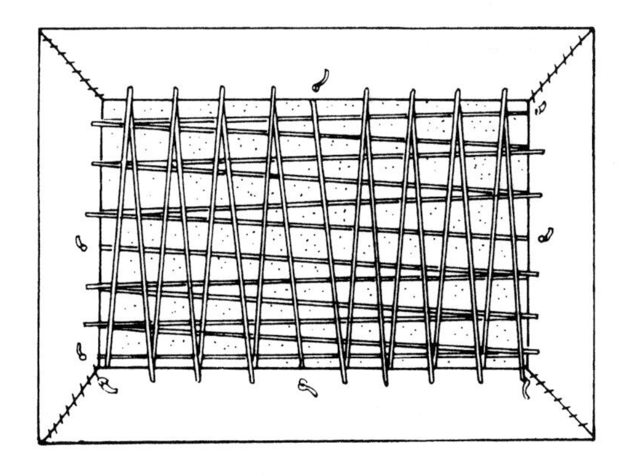

- Lay the embroidery face down, with the cardboard centred on top; fold over the edges of the fabric on opposite sides, making mitred folds at the corners, and lace across, using strong thread. Repeat on the other two sides. Finally, pull up the fabric firmly over the cardboard. Overstitch the mitred corners.

Bay Tree Hanging

This bay tree in a terracotta pot is buzzing with beaded bees! The trunk can easily be lengthened or shortened, to suit your individual needs, and you can make up the finished embroidery either as a bellpull or as a wall hanging.

BAY TREE HANGING

YOU WILL NEED

For a hanging measuring approximately 55cm × 17cm (22in × 6½in):

72.5cm × 23cm (29in × 9in) of of 28-count evenweave fabric in forget-me-not blue
57.5cm × 19cm (23in × 7½in) of matching or toning backing fabric
Stranded embroidery cotton in the colours listed in the panel.
Gold thread (DMC Fil d'or or a similar thread)
No24 tapestry needle
Black and yellow seed beads (optional)
Beading needle
Sewing threads to match the fabric and the bead colours
Two pieces of 12mm (½in) dowel, each 22cm (8½in) long, sanded smooth and varnished, for hangers
End stops for the hangers, if desired
1m (1yd) of ribbon, 12mm (½in) wide

Note The bees may either be decorated with beading or simply cross stitched. If you do not wish to make your own hangers, you can purchase ready-made ones from craft suppliers (see page 40). If you are making a longer or shorter hanging, adjust the fabric quantities accordingly.

•

THE EMBROIDERY

Prepare the edges of the fabric in the usual way (see page 4) and mark the centre lines with basting stitches. Set the fabric in a frame (see page 5). If you wish to lengthen the trunk, you can do so at the point marked on the chart by simply repeating a random section of the trunk until you reach the required length. If you wish to shorten the trunk, just remove the required amount from the section indicated on the chart.

Using two strands of cotton in the needle, and taking each stitch over two threads of the fabric, complete all the cross stitches. If you decide to cross stitch the bees, use the black and yellow threads used elsewhere in the design and follow the chart in

TOP

BAY TREE ▶	DMC	ANCHOR	MADEIRA
▽ Light trunk brown	372	853	2110
○ Trunk brown	370	855	2111
✱ Dark trunk brown	3021	905	1904
◇ Dark ribbon yellow	741	304	0201
+ Ribbon yellow	742	302	0113
● Pale ribbon yellow	744	301	0112
▲ Dark terracotta	3777	20	0811
⦸ Terracotta	919	1004	0313
X Pale terracotta	922	1003	0311
△ Lighest green	907	255	1410
□ Bright green	906	256	1411
◆ Medium green	904	258	1413
▼ Dark green	890	1044	1314
■ Black	310	403	Black

Note: backstitch the bees' wings in gold thread, and the stings in either gold or black, using one strand of thread in the needle.

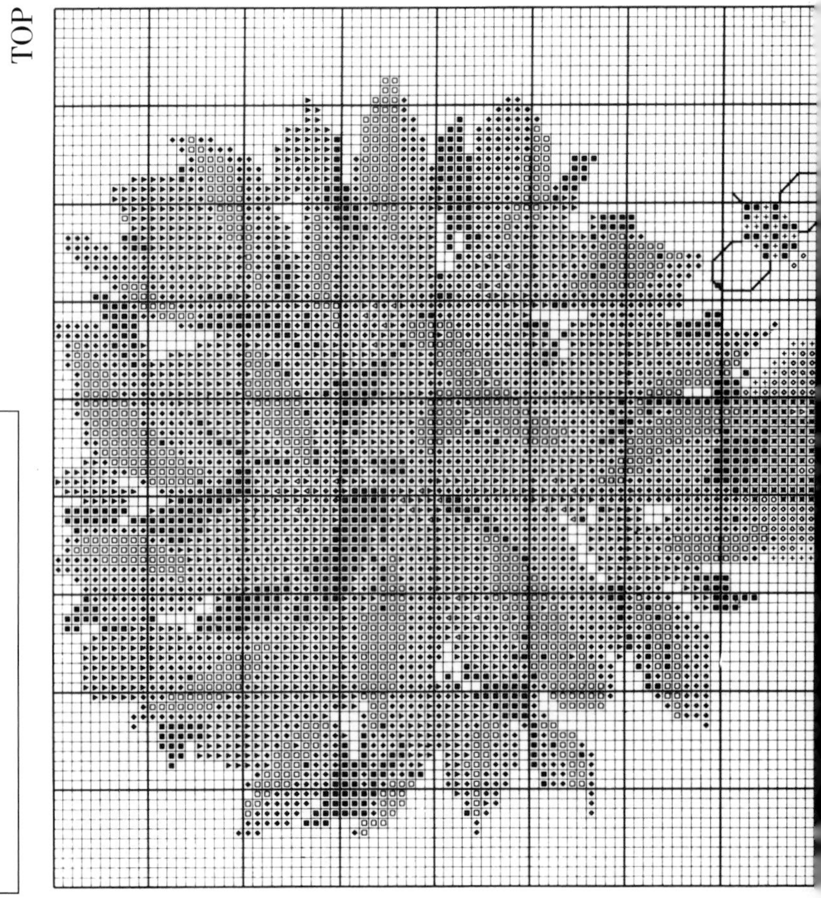

the usual way. If you decide to use beads, follow the chart but instead of a cross stitch, sew a bead into each square, using a half cross stitch (see page 7). To ensure that the beads 'sit' on the fabric evenly, these diagonal stitches must all be worked in the same direction on any bee; however, different bees can face different directions.

When using the gold thread for the bees' wings, cut only short pieces to prevent it splitting or wearing as you sew. This type of thread can sometimes twist easily, so the shorter your thread, the more manageable it will be. Backstitch the wings, using only one strand of gold thread in the needle. When the embroidery is finished, iron on the reverse side over a soft towel to prevent damage to the beads and threads.

MAKING THE HANGING

Trim the sides of the embroidery to extend 2.5cm (1in) beyond the nearest stitches; trim the bottom to leave 11.5cm (4½in) beyond the last row of stitches, and the top to leave 9.5cm (3¾in) above the topmost stitches.

Turn in the long edges by 12mm (½in) and press. Lightly catchstitch the turnings to the back of the embroidery. On each short edge, make a 6mm (¼in) turning, then make another turning, 4cm (1½in) deep – this should be sufficient to carry the dowel. Baste and neatly hem in place.

Make a 1.5mm (⅝in) turning to the back down each side of the backing fabric and at the top and bottom edges. Press and then pin the backing to the back of the embroidery. Neatly slipstitch in place, leaving the side edges of the casing open.

If the dowel lengths are rough, they may need to be lightly sanded smooth and then varnished before use. Allow the varnish to dry, and then slip the dowel lengths into the top and bottom casings. To finish, tie the ribbon to the ends of the top dowel to make a hanging loop. You may wish to add end stops to the dowel lengths; alternatively, you may find that you need a few dabs of glue to help to secure the ribbon ends firmly to the dowel.

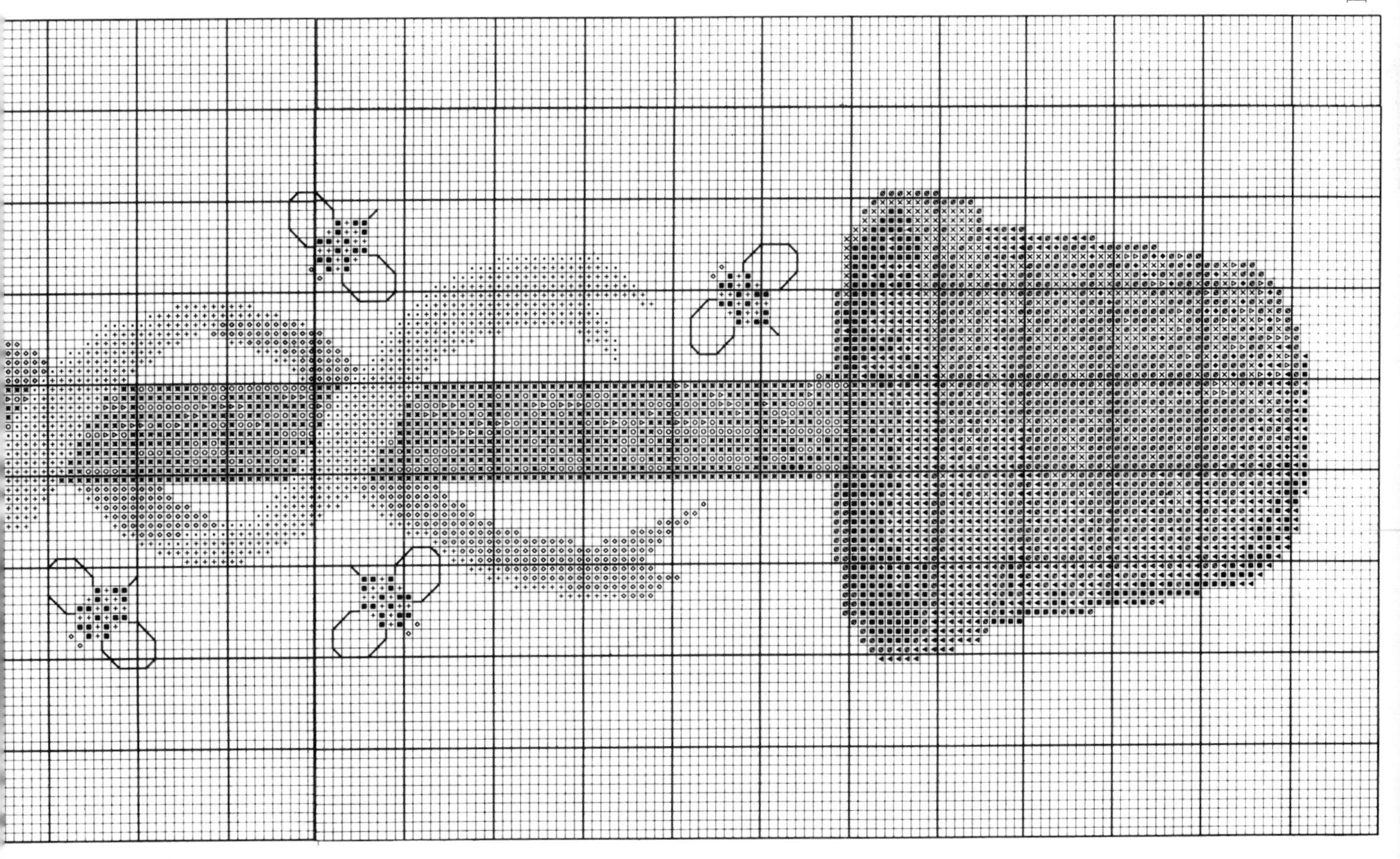

Lavender Bags and Trinket Box

The scent of lavender will permeate cupboards and drawers and its beauty decorate your room all year round. These simple designs can be adapted to almost any project.

LAVENDER BAGS AND TRINKET BOX

YOU WILL NEED

For a lavender bag, measuring approximately 14cm × 7.5cm (5¼in × 3in):

21cm × 19.5cm (8½in × 7½in) of 28-count, violet evenweave fabric
Stranded cotton in the colours given in the panel
No24 tapestry needle
30cm (12in) of violet ribbon, 1cm (⅜in) wide
Sewing thread to match the fabric
Dried lavender or pot pourri, for filling

For a drawer scenter, measuring 10cm (4in) square:

15cm (6in) square of evenweave fabric, plus needle, threads, and filling, as above
12.5cm (5in) square of printed cotton, for the back
17.5cm (7in) of violet ribbon, 1cm (⅜in) wide
Matching sewing thread

For the make-up bag, measuring 16cm × 12.5cm (6¼in × 5in):

Ready-made bag in 28-count evenweave (the colour used is English Rose), for suppliers see page 40
Needle and threads, as above

For the trinket box, with a lid measuring 5.5cm (2⅛in) in diameter:

15cm (6in) square of 14-count, white Aida fabric
Needle and threads, as above
Trinket box, for suppliers see page 40

Note If you are only stitching the Lavender Row design, you will not require dark pink embroidery cotton; for Lavender Bunch, you will not require silver green, and for Lavender Posy, you will not require pale pink, dark green and dark pink.

•

LAVENDER BAG

The diagram shows the trimmed fabric, but the fabric quantity gives an additional allowance of 2.5cm (1in) all around. Using basting stitches, mark off the work area, 3cm (1¼in) up from the lower edge of the fabric and the same in from each side. Mark down the centre of the fabric – the right-hand side is the work area. Mark a horizontal line 7.5cm (3in) up from the lower line of basting, and a second line 1cm (⅜in) above it. Mark the centre of the enclosed work area with basting stitches and set the fabric in a hoop.

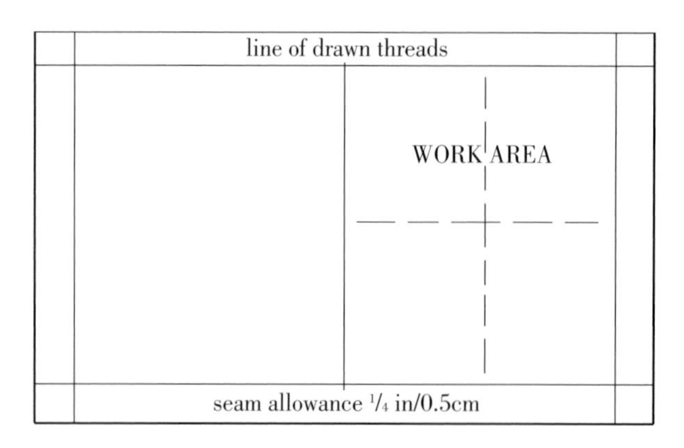

Embroider the design, using two strands of thread in the needle for the cross stitches and a single strand for the backstitch and taking each stitch over two threads of the fabric.

When you have finished the embroidery, trim the fabric to measure 16cm × 14.5cm (6½in × 5½in) and carefully remove all horizontal threads from between the two upper horizontal lines of basting stitches. Fold the fabric down the centre, right sides together, and stitch the bottom and side edges, taking a 6mm (¼in) seam allowance. Turn the bag right side out and remove horizontal threads from the top 12mm (½in), to make a fringe. Thread ribbon through the drawn-thread area, over 10 and then under 5 threads, starting and finishing at the seam. Fill the bag with lavender, then draw the ribbon and tie it in a bow.

DRAWER SCENTER

Mark the centre of the fabric with basting stitches and embroider the design, using two strands of thread in the needle for the cross stitches and a single strand for the backstitch and taking each stitch over two threads of the fabric. Trim the finished embroidery to measure 12.5cm (5in) square. Fold the ribbon in half and pin it to lie over the front side, with the loop to the centre and the ends at one corner. With right sides together, lay the printed cotton over the embroidery and loop and stitch around three sides, leaving a gap of 5cm (2in) in the remaining side and taking a 12mm (½in) seam allowance. Turn the fabric right side out; fill with lavender, and then stitch the opening together neatly.

MAKE-UP BAG

Mark the centre of your work in the usual way. You cannot use a hoop, but this does not matter for a small piece of embroidery. Embroider the design, as for the lavender bag, repeating stems until you reach the required width (stop about 6mm/ 1/4in short of the seams). When you have finished, stitch the lining together and push it back inside the pouch. As a finishing touch, you can tie a short length of ribbon through the tongue of the zip.

TRINKET BOX

Mark the centre of the fabric with basting stitches and set in a small hoop or hold it in the hand Embroider the design, using two strands of thread in the needle throughout. Using the template provided and with the basting stitches as guidelines, mark the shape of the lid on the fabric and cut it out. Remove the basting stitches and mount the fabric in the lid, following the manufacturer's instructions.

LAVENDER	DMC	ANCHOR	MADEIRA
◆ Silver grey	452	232	1807
■ Violet	792	177	0903
▼ Lavender	793	176	0902
X Lilac	341	117	0901
◇ Pale pink	224	894	0813
● Dark green	924	879	1205
⦸ Silver green	926	838	1310
□ Dark pink	3733	75	0605

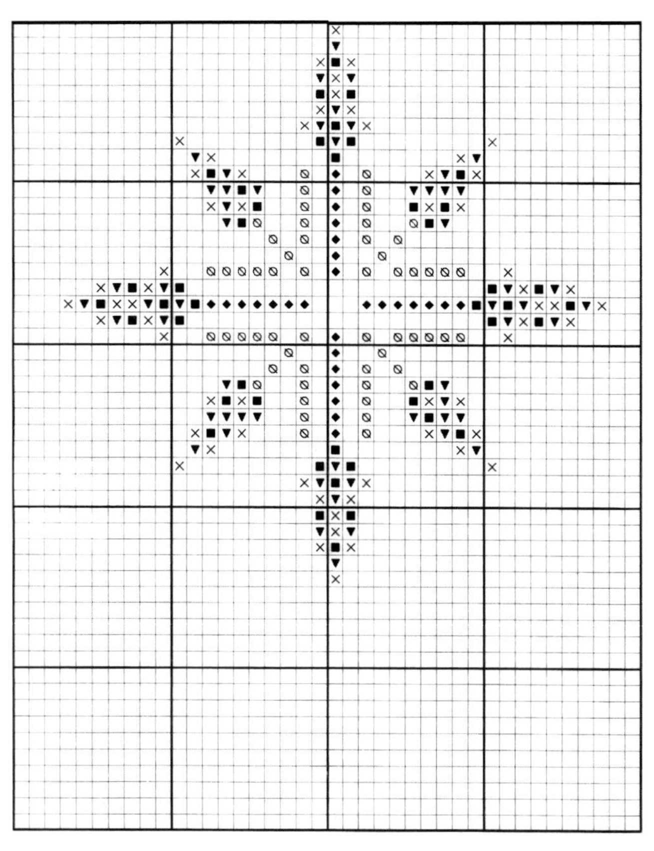

LAVENDER POSY

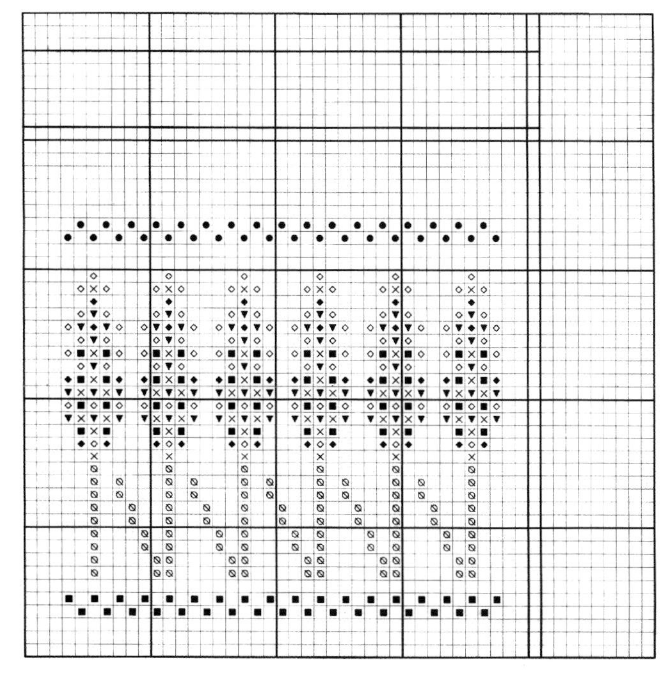

LAVENDER ROW

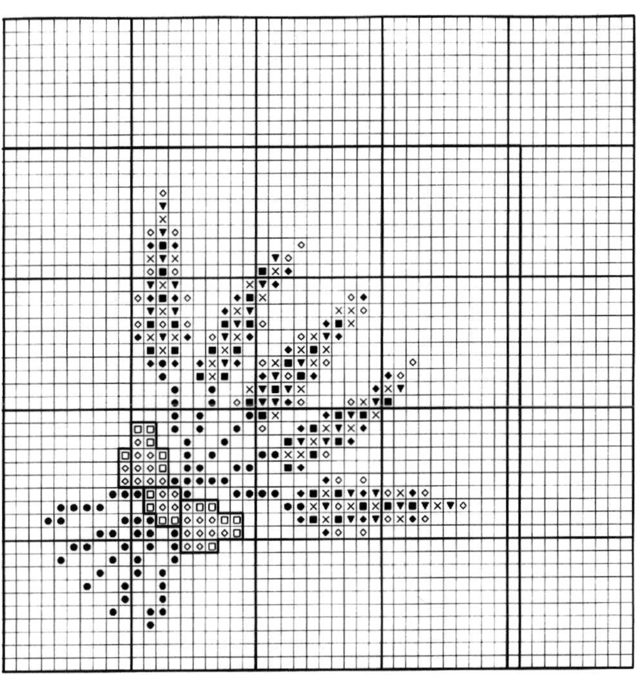

LAVENDER BUNCH

Guest Room Set

Garlands of marjoram and savory edge the towels, and a pillow embroidered with sage, thyme, sorrel and chamomile and filled with sweet-scented leaves ensures a good night's sleep. A bookmark makes a charming parting gift.

GUEST ROOM SET

YOU WILL NEED

For the pillow, measuring approximately 27.5cm (11in) square (excluding the lace trim):

One panel of damask fabric, 30cm (12in) square, with a circle of 11-count Aida weave, 10cm (4in) in diameter, at the centre (for suppliers see page 40)
30cm (12in) square of fabric of your choice, for the back
Stranded embroidery cotton in the colours given in the appropriate panel
No24 tapestry needle
130cm (52in) of gathered lace trim, 4cm (1½in) deep
Sewing cotton to match fabric
25cm (10in) square of net or fine muslin
Small bunch of dried herbs or a handful of pot pourri or dried lavender
30cm (12in) square cushion pad (for a well-filled effect)

For the towels:

16-count, white Aida band, 5cm (2in) wide, to the width of your towel, plus 2.5cm (1in)
Stranded embroidery cotton in the colours given in the appropriate panel
No24 tapestry needle
Towel of your choice
Sewing thread

For the bookmark, measuring approximately 19.5cm × 5cm (7¾in × 2in):

40cm (16in) of Aida band
Stranded embroidery cotton, needle and thread, as above

•

THE EMBROIDERY

For the pillow, first prepare the fabric by basting a narrow hem around the edge of the damask to prevent it fraying while you work. Mark the centre of the Aida circle with horizontal and vertical lines of basting stitches. Mount the panel with the Aida fabric centred in an embroidery hoop.

Count out from the centre to start embroidering the design at a convenient point, and use three strands of cotton in the needle throughout. When you have finished, remove all basting stitches (including the temporary hem) and gently steam press the embroidery on the wrong side.

For the towels, either turn a small hem or bind the raw edges at each end of the band with masking tape to prevent fraying. Mark the centre of the band with a vertical line of basting stitches. Use two strands of thread in the needle throughout and work from the centre outwards to ensure that the repeats will be evenly spread along the band.

To embroider the bookmark, mark across the band at the centre with a line of basting stitches and embroider one half of the band only (the front of the bookmark). Start at a point 6mm (¼in) away from this marked centre line and follow the chart from the edge until you have embroidered as far as the fourth pink flower (use the photograph as a guide).

MAKING THE PILLOW

Check that both front and back fabrics measure 30cm (12in) square; trim if necessary. Lay the embroidered front panel face up and pin the lace around the edge of the panel, with the decorative edge facing inwards and the straight, gathered edge just within the 12mm (½in) seam allowance. Ease the lace around the corners and trim the short ends, if necessary, before joining them with a neat French seam. Machine the lace in place.

Keeping the lace tucked inside, place the front and back sections with right sides together and machine around the edge, taking a 12mm (½in) seam allowance and leaving a gap of 15cm (6in) at the centre of one side. Turn the cover right side out and insert the cushion pad. For a scented pillow, tie dried herbs, pot pourri or dried lavender in a piece of net and slip this in, next to the pad. Slipstitch across the gap to close it.

THE TOWELS

Remove any basting stitches and, if necessary, iron the band on the wrong side, using a steam iron. Covering the area that has no pile, pin the Aida band across the width of the towel; start from the centre and turn under the raw edges at each end. Machine or handstitch the band to the towel.

THE BOOKMARK

With right sides together, fold the band in half across the marked centre line and machine or handstitch the raw edges at the bottom into a point. Trim and then turn right side out, gently pushing out the point. Pin the long sides together and join with a small running stitch, following the Aida squares.

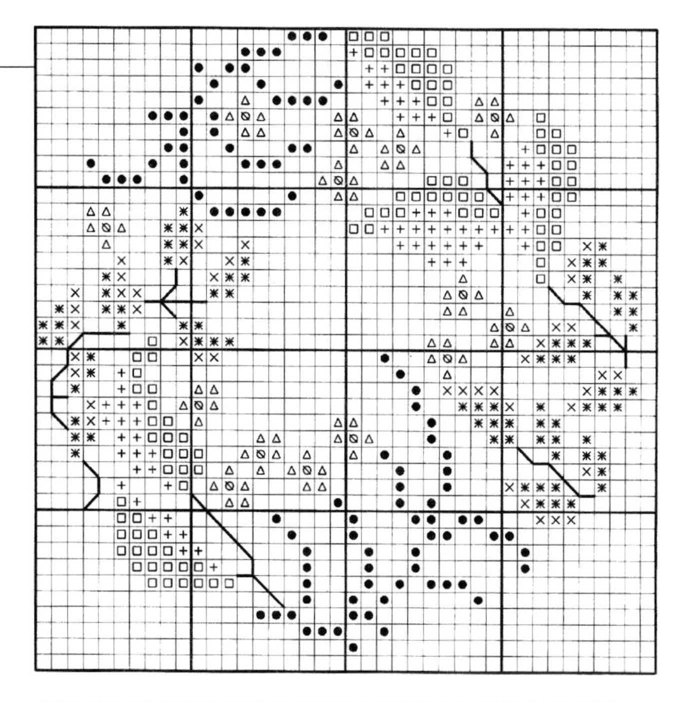

BAND OF FLOWERS ▼

Pink colourway	DMC	ANCHOR	MADEIRA
○ Dark pink	3350	59	0603
▽ Medium pink	3733	75	0605
+ Pale pink	224	894	0813
⦸ Stone	370	855	2112
● Dark green	731	281	1613
✳ Light green	733	280	1611
◆ Dark blue	792	177	0903
□ Medium blue	793	176	0902
X Light blue	341	117	0901
△ Yellow	744	301	0112

Note: backstitch the stems in stone and the flowers in yellow, using two strands of thread in the needle.

BAND OF FLOWERS ▼

Violet colourway	DMC	ANCHOR	MADEIRA
○ Violet	792	177	0903
▽ Lavender	793	176	0902
+ Lilac	341	117	0901
⦸ Straw	676	891	2012
● Olive	370	855	2112
✳ Light olive	372	853	2110
◆ Teal	924	683	1706
□ Light teal	926	838	1707
X Silver green	927	837	1708
△ Ecru	Ecru	590	Ecru

Note: backstitch the stems in straw and the flowers in ecru, using two strands of thread in the needle.

SLEEP WELL PILLOW ▲

	DMC	ANCHOR	MADEIRA
● Olive green	372	853	2110
✳ Dark gold	676	891	2012
X Gold	677	300	2014
▽ Light pink	255	968	0814
⦸ Dark pink	224	894	0813
□ Dark silver green	927	838	1707
+ Light silver green	928	837	1708

Note: backstitch stems in dark silver green or dark gold, as appropriate, using three strands of thread in the needle.

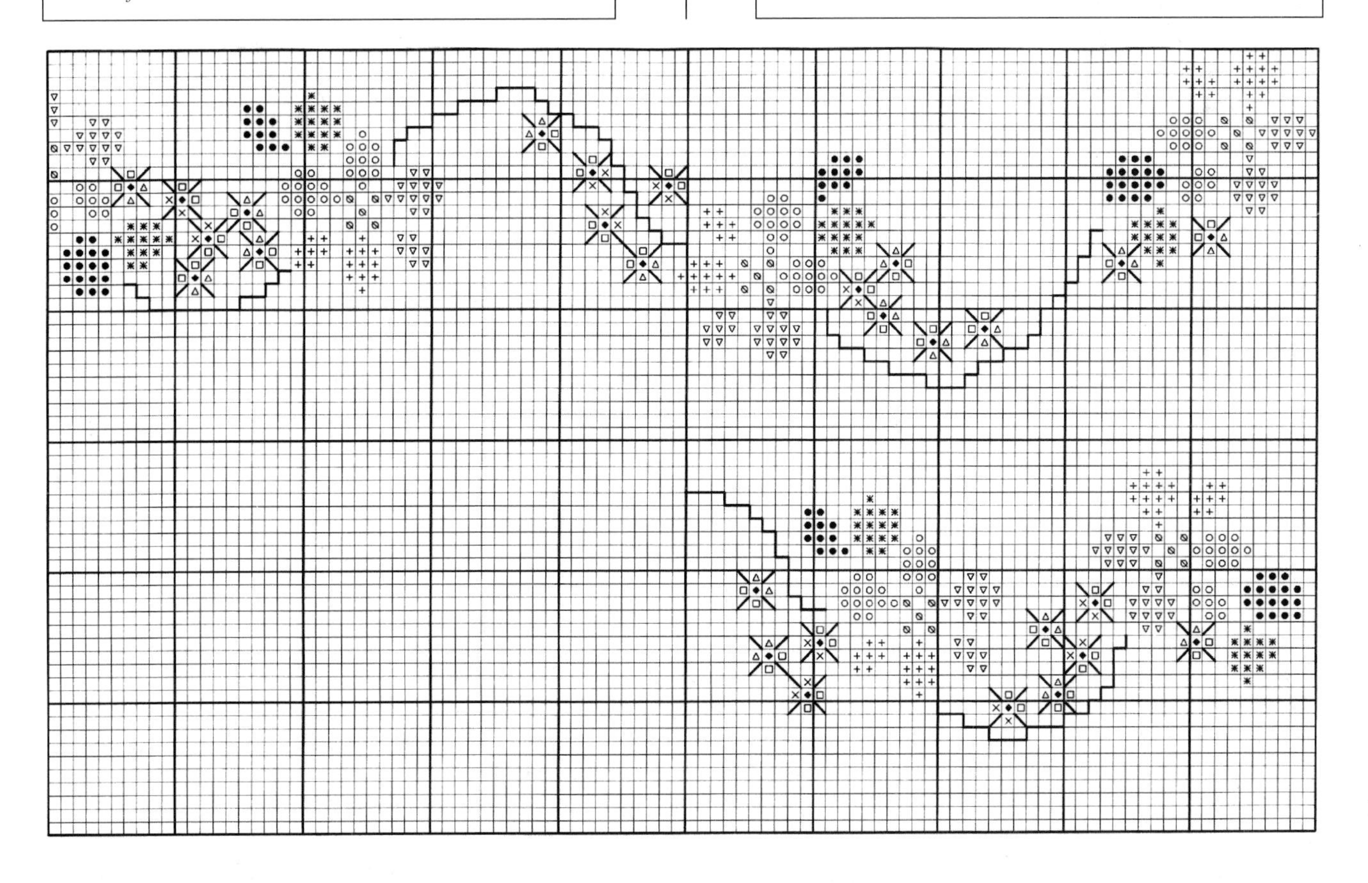

Conservatory Cushion

This colourful collection of herbs in flower would look equally good as a cushion cover, a wall hanging, or a set of individual pictures to scatter around your home. They would also make charming greetings cards for special friends.

CONSERVATORY CUSHION

YOU WILL NEED

For the cushion cover, measuring 42.5cm (17in) square:

30cm (12in) square of 16-count, cream Aida fabric
Stranded embroidery cotton in the colours listed in the panel
No24 tapestry needle
Cream printed cotton: two pieces, each 45cm (18in) square, and one piece 45cm × 10cm (18in × 14in)
Green printed cotton: four strips 4cm × 27cm (1½in × 10½in) and four strips 4.5cm × 45cm (1¾in × 18in)
Matching cream sewing cotton
Three press fastenings (optional)
Cushion pad 45cm (18in) square, for a well-filled effect

•

THE EMBROIDERY

Prepare the edges of the fabric (see page 4), marking the centre both ways with lines of basting stitches in a light-coloured thread, and set it in a frame. Start by stitching the gold border square of the centre panel (Thyme), then count out and stitch the remaining eight border squares and the outer square in gold and then dark green. Cross stitch with two strands of thread in the needle throughout.

When you have established the borders, stitch each panel in turn. You may find it helpful to mark the centre of each individual panel with basting

CONSERVATORY ▶ CUSHION	DMC	ANCHOR	MADEIRA
▼ Dark grey	414	235	1714
◇ Light grey	452	232	1807
◆ Gold	782	308	2212
▽ Yellow	726	295	0109
+ Pale pink	224	894	0813
X Light purple	327	100	0805
▲ Purple	550	102	0714
△ Medium pink/ coral	3733	75	0605
■ Bottle green	890	1044	1314
⦸ Dark pink	3350	59	0603
□ Bright green	906	256	1411
● Dark olive	731	281	1613
✳ Medium olive	733	280	1611
○ Light olive	370	855	2112
• White	White	1	White

Note: backstitch the dill border in bottle green, using one strand of thread in the needle.

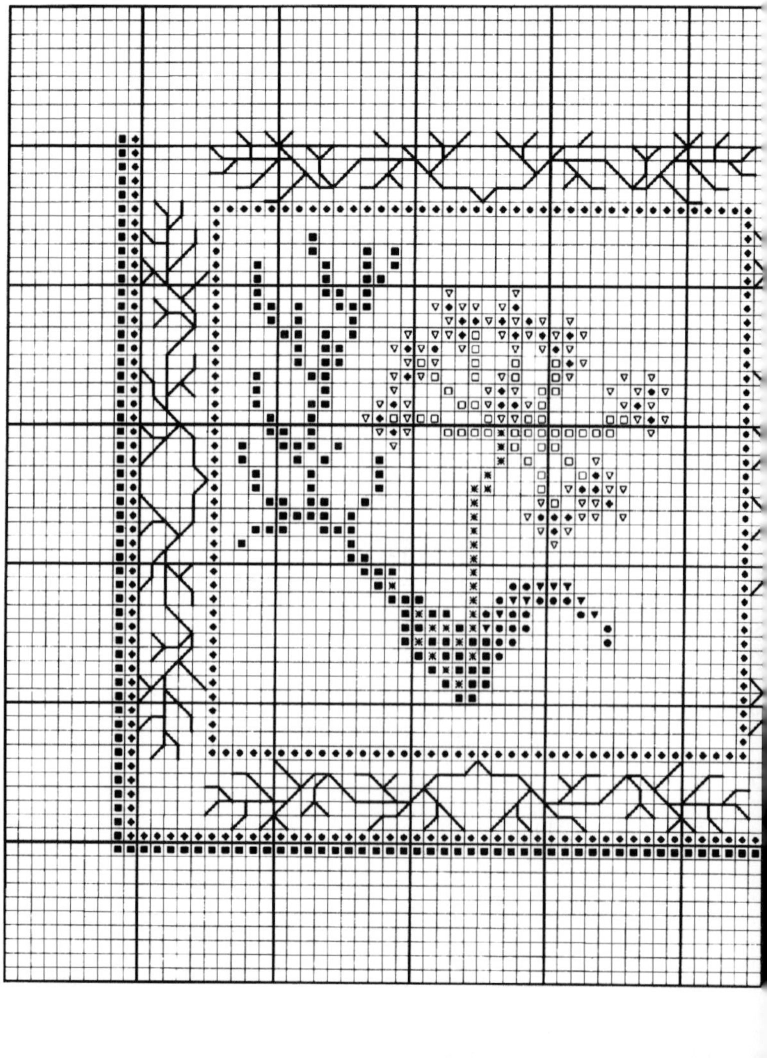

stitches, or count carefully to the centre and stitch from the centre outwards. When you have finished all the cross stitching, backstitch the dill that runs between the borders, using one strand only in the needle, for a suitably feathery effect.

When you have finished the embroidery, take the fabric from the frame and remove all basting stitches. Press lightly on the wrong side, using a steam iron.

MAKING THE COVER

Take the shorter green strips and, with wrong sides together, press each in half lengthways. Lay each in turn on the right side of the embroidered fabric, with the folded edge running along one side of the green outer border. Taking an allowance of six Aida blocks (1cm/3/8in) out from the green border, stitch each strip to the fabric, stopping six Aida blocks beyond the level of the last green stitch at each end, so that the ends of the strips are free. When strips have been attached to each edge, trim the Aida back to about 6mm (1/4in) beyond the stitching, and press the border strips away from the fabric, with all seam allowances lying under the embroidery. Turn under and arrange the raw edges at the corners, to leave neatly folded, sharp corners.

Take the prepared panel and centre it over the right side of one of the squares of cream fabric. Stitching in the seamline between the Aida and the green border, stitch the panel to the cream square.

Take the remaining, longer strips of green fabric and turn under 12mm (1/2in) down each short edge and press. With wrong sides together, fold and press each strip in half lengthways. Lay each strip in turn on the right side of the fabric, with the folded edge inward and raw edges matching. Taking a 12mm (1/2in) seam allowance, stitch the strips around the

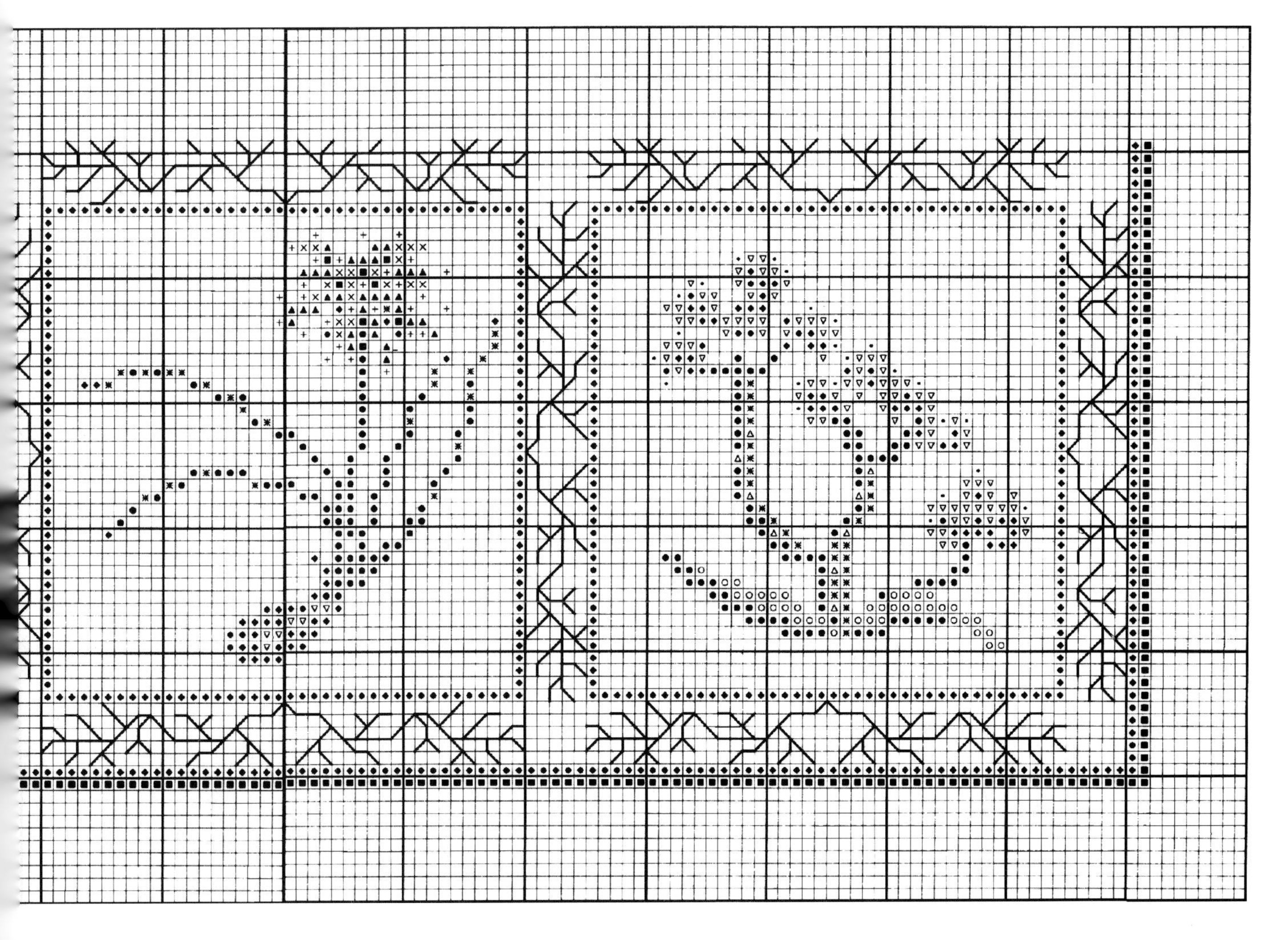

edge of the fabric, so that the short folded ends stop 12mm (1/2in) short of the raw edges of the cream fabric at each end.

Take the two remaining pieces of cream fabric and turn under and stitch a double 12mm (1/2in) hem along one long side of each. Take the narrow strip and, with right sides together and the raw edges matching the raw edges at one side of the front cover, lay it on the front cushion cover. Take the second, larger piece and, again with right sides together, lay it over the cushion front, with the hemmed edge overlapping the narrower strip. Stitch all around the outer edge, taking a 12mm (1/2in) seam allowance and stitching along the line attaching the green border strips (take care that these lie inwards and will stand free when the cover is turned right side out).

Turn the cover right side out and insert the cushion pad. You may choose to stitch press fastenings to secure the envelope opening, but these may not be necessary.

CHERVIL	CALENDULA	CHAMOMILE
BORAGE	THYME	MINT
FENNEL	CHIVES	LOVAGE

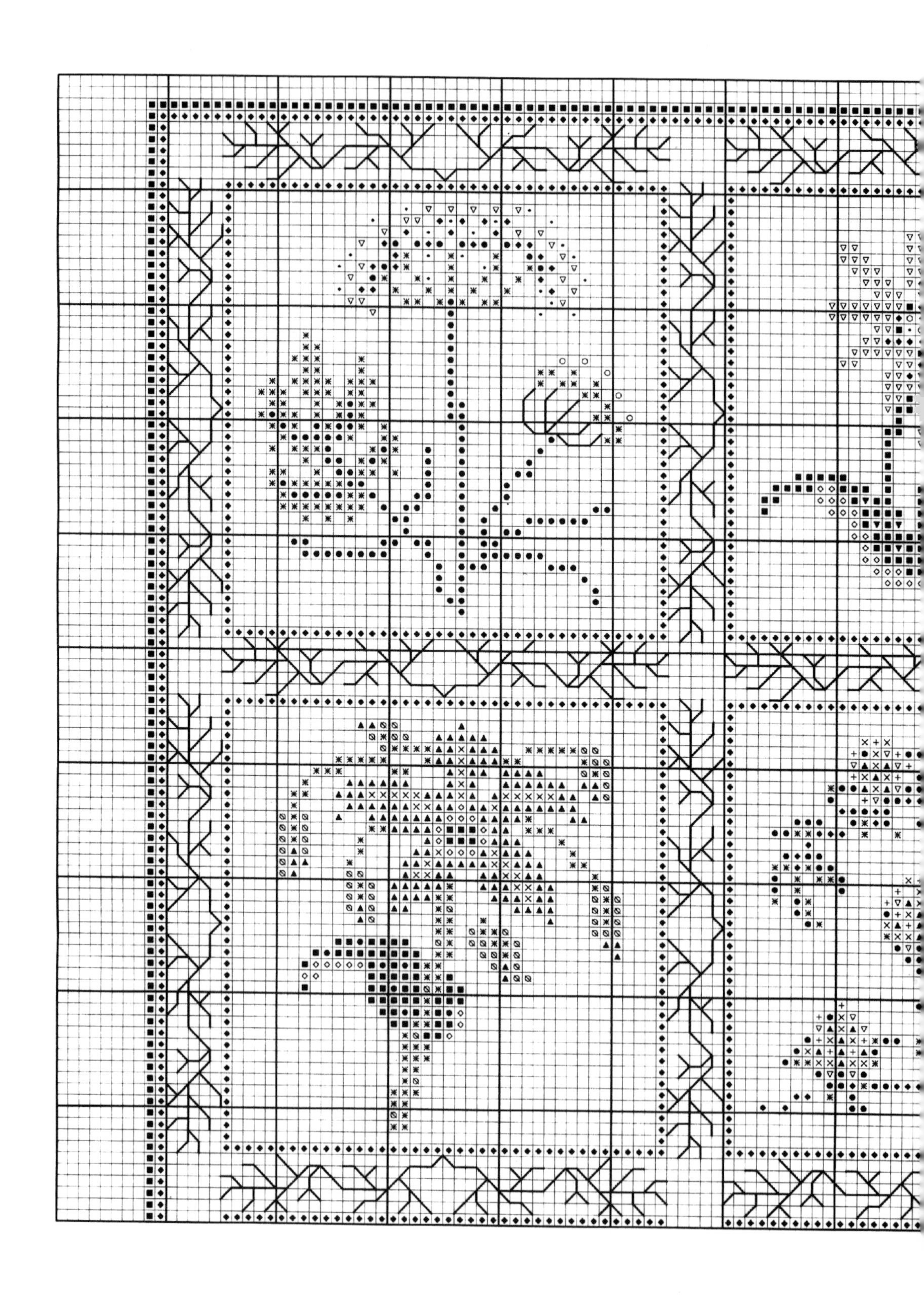

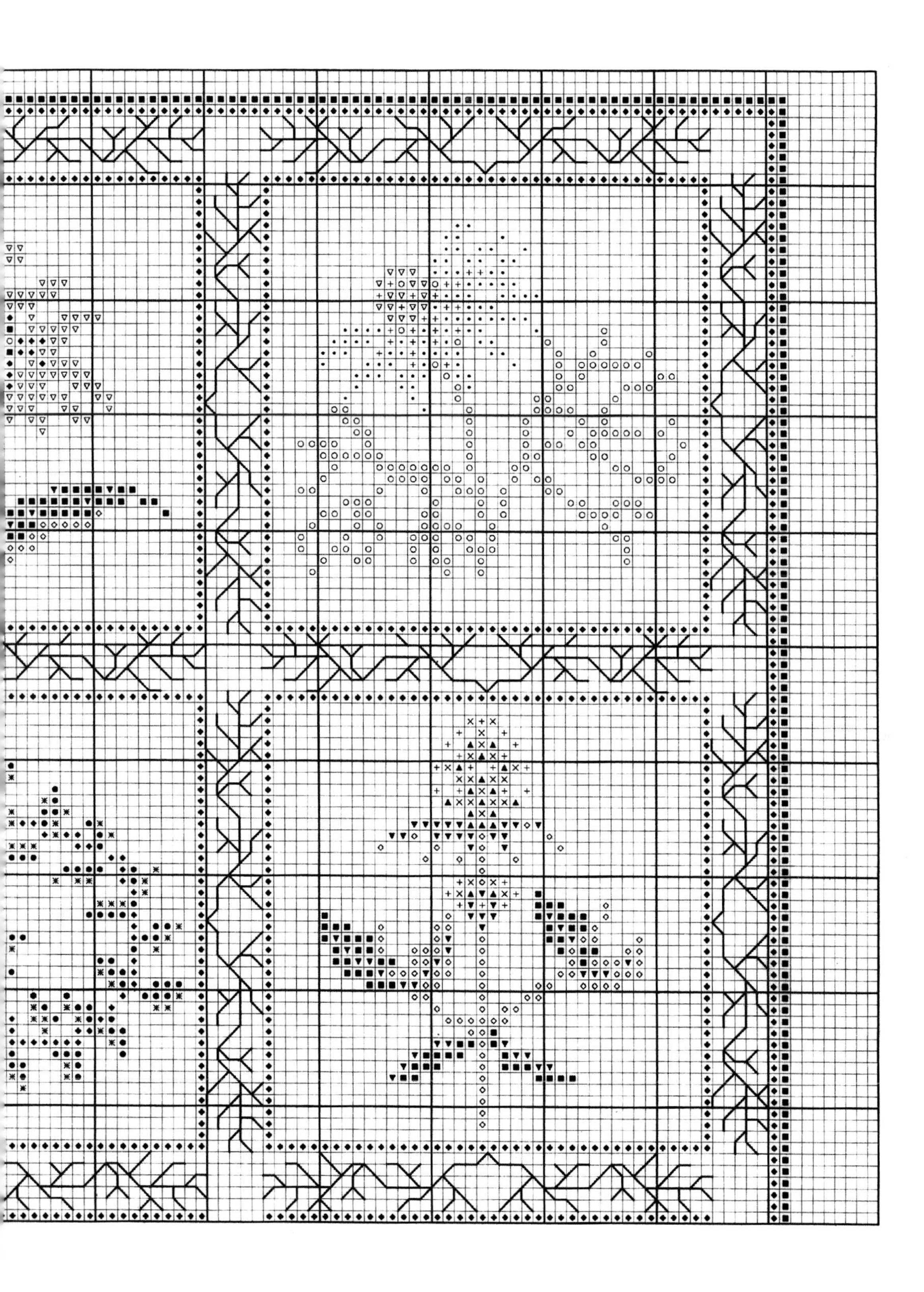

Anna

For a Golden Table

Add a golden sparkle to your table on special occasions, such as wedding anniversaries, with a set of either basil or nasturtium napkins, or a mixture of both, and nasturtium place cards, all stitched in gold thread.

FOR A GOLDEN TABLE

YOU WILL NEED

For each napkin, of either the basil or nasturtium design, measuring 37.5cm (15in) square:

Either a ready-made napkin in a plain colour of your choice or a 40cm (16in) square of cotton, cotton/polyester or linen fabric
DMC Fil d'or or a similar gold embroidery thread
14-count waste canvas – 8cm × 10cm for each basil napkin or a 10cm (4in) square cut diagonally in half for two nasturtium napkins
No 6 crewel needle
Sewing thread
Laundry spray
Tweezers or fine jeweller's pliers
Gold tassel (optional)

For each place card, measuring 10cm (4in) each way (maximum height):

10cm × 14cm (4in × 5½in) of Aida plus (or 14-count Aida and iron-on fabric stiffener cut to measure)
DMC Fil d'or or a similar gold embroidery thread
No 24 tapestry needle

•

THE NAPKINS

If you are making your own napkins, first turn under and press a double 6mm (¼in) hem all around and machine stitch, close to the folded edge. If you are embroidering the basil napkin, baste the waste canvas at a 45 degree angle to one corner, and mark the centre of the canvas as you would if you were embroidering a piece of Aida fabric.

For a nasturtium napkin, baste the right angle of the canvas to the right angle of machine stitching at one corner; count up from the corner to start stitching the centre of the nasturtium flower 4.5cm (1½in) in from the corner. Embroider the design through both the canvas and the napkin fabric, using two strands of gold thread. Use very short lengths of this special thread to prevent it wearing out or becoming tarnished.

FINISHING THE NAPKIN

When the embroidery is complete, trim the excess canvas to about 12mm (½in) around the edges of your stitching. Now dampen the remainder with a laundry spray. The canvas will become damp and sticky. While it is in this state, gently but firmly pull the canvas threads from underneath the gold thread. It is a good idea to practise on those threads around the edge that have no embroidered stitches over them; in this way you will familiarize yourself with the feel of the damp canvas before tackling your precious stitches

Once all the canvas has been removed, your gold work will gleam on the fabric! Leave the napkins to dry naturally, or press on the reverse side with a clean cloth, over a soft towel to protect the stitching. These napkins can be hand washed, or machine washed on a gentle cycle. If you use starch, spray onto the reverse side only.

For the basil napkin, hand sew a running stitch along all four edges, using the gold thread and following the machine-stitched hem as a guide. Again using the gold thread, weave a second line under these stitches, producing a wavy line around the edge.

If you choose to finish each napkin with a tassel, use only a few stitches and make sure that it can easily be removed for laundering, when necessary.

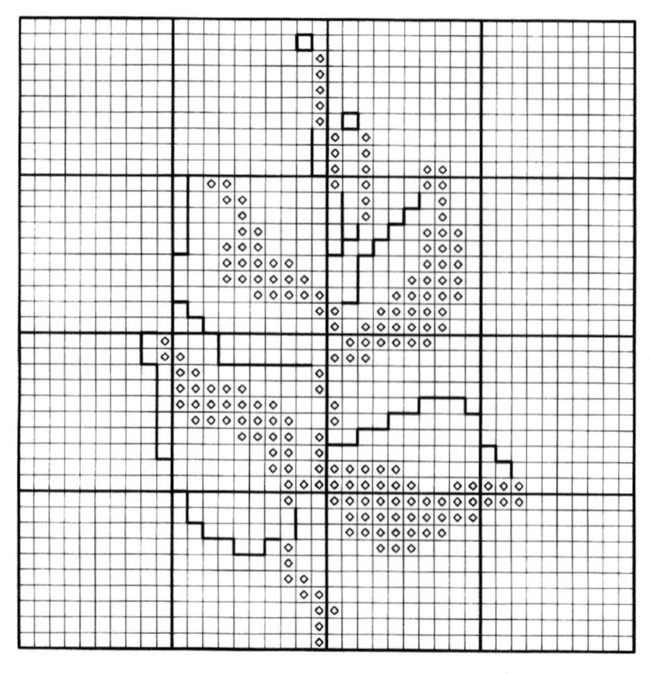

BASIL NAPKIN

NASTURTIUM NAPKIN

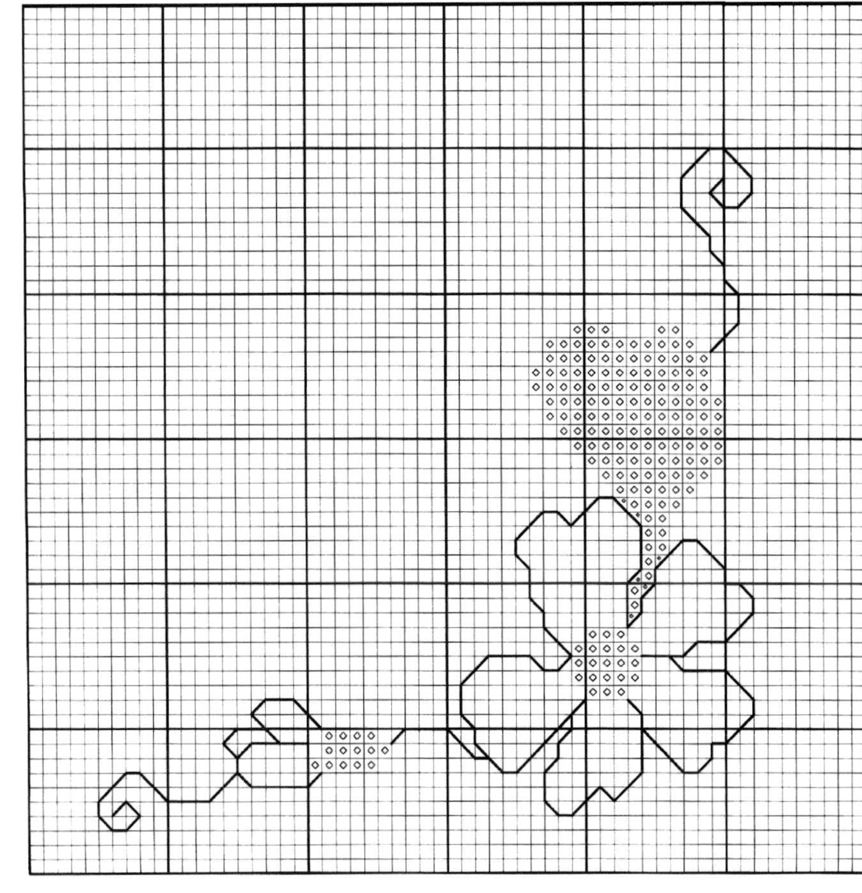

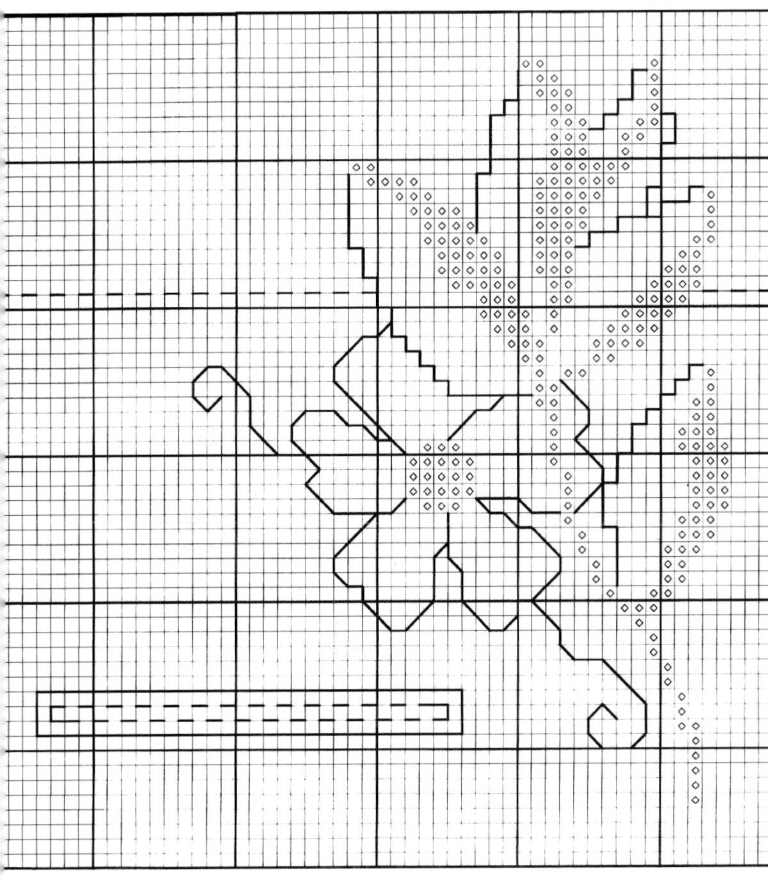

PLACE CARDS

Stitch the design, following the chart in the usual way. If you are using Aida plus, it is not necessary to mount this in a hoop. When the stitching is finished, fold along the line marked on the chart.

Carefully cut from this fold around the leaves, stopping when you reach the fold on the other side of them. Now cut the slot as illustrated. Re-fold the card along the crease, leaving the cut-out part standing free. Iron on the reverse side.

Write the name of your guest on a piece of card and slip it into the slot. In this way you will be able to use your place cards over and over again.

NASTURTIUM PLACE CARD

Assisi Gift Collection

The background is stitched and the motifs left open in Assisi work. Here, this traditional style is used to feature a sprig of mint, a snip of chervil and a chicory flower. The background can easily shrink or expand to fit different objects.

ASSISI GIFT COLLECTION

YOU WILL NEED

For the mint trinket box, with an oval lid measuring 5cm × 7.3cm (2in × 2⁷/₈in):

10cm × 12cm (4in × 4³/₄in) of 16-count, cream Aida fabric
Stranded embroidery cotton as given in the appropriate panel
No 24 tapestry needle
Trinket box (for suppliers, see page 40)

For the mint greeting card, with an aperture measuring 9cm × 6cm (3¹/₂in × 2¹/₂in):

11.5cm × 8¹/₂cm (4¹/₂in × 3¹/₂in) of 14-count, cream Aida fabric
Stranded embroidery cotton and needle, as above
Greetings card (for suppliers, see page 40)

For the chicory flower greetings card, with an aperture measuring 6cm (2¹/₂in) square:

8.5cm (3¹/₂in) square of 14-count, white Aida fabric
Standard embroidery cotton and needle, as above
Greetings card (for suppliers, see page 40)

For the chervil paperweight, measuring 7cm (2³/₄in) in diameter:

10cm (4in) square of 14-count, white Aida fabric
Standard embroidery cotton and needle, as above
Paperweight (for suppliers, see page 40)

•

THE EMBROIDERY

For each design, mark the centre of the fabric both ways with lines of basting stitches (see page 4) and either work with the fabric held in the hand or in a small hoop (see page 5). Using one strand of embroidery cotton in the needle for the mint design, and two strands for the chicory or chervil designs, complete all the backstitching. Using two strands of embroidery cotton in the needle for all designs, cross stitch around the outer boundary of your chosen design, and then fill in the gap between the outer line and the inner line of backstitching that outlines the motif.

GREETINGS CARDS

Trim the embroidered fabric to fit the inside of the card and remove the basting stitches. Position the embroidery centrally behind the cut-out, then fold over the front flap of the card and press (you may need to add a small piece of double-sided tape to secure it).

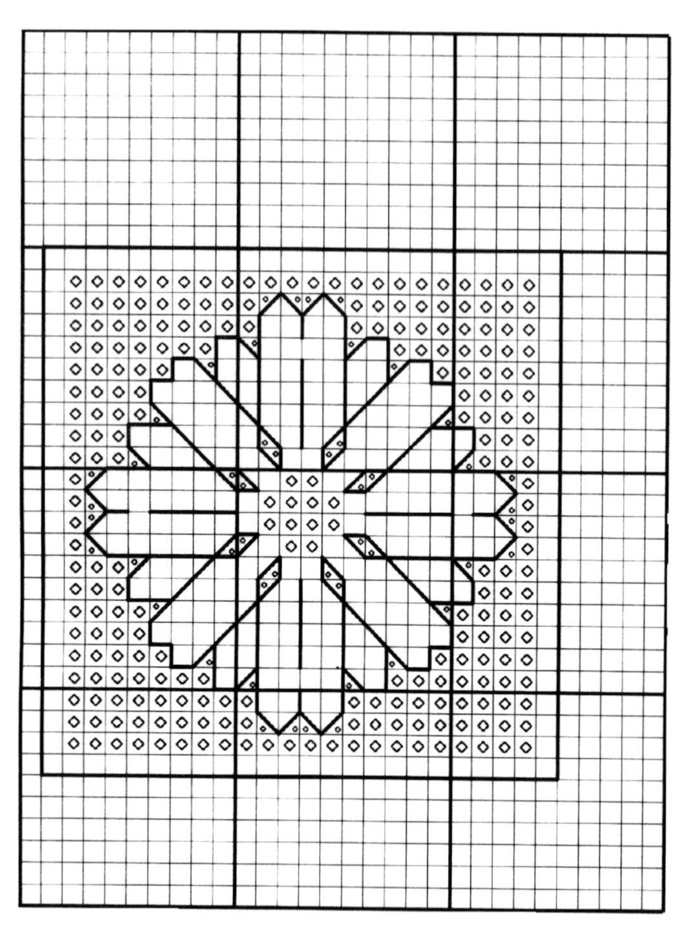

CHICORY

ASSISI GIFTS			
Mint	DMC	ANCHOR	MADEIRA
● Green	3345	263	1507
Chervil			
▲ Purple	327	112	0713
Chicory			
◇ Light brown	435	308	2212

MINT

TRINKET BOX AND PAPERWEIGHT

Mark both ways across the centre of the template provided. Lay the embroidery face down on a clean surface and centre the template over it, matching the pencil lines and the basted centre lines. Lightly draw around the outline and then cut the fabric to shape. Remove the basting stitches and complete the assembly, following the manufacturer's instructions.

CHERVIL

Jar Covers and Labels

Pots of home-made apple jelly with either sage or mint, oil flavoured with rosemary, and tarragon vinegar – all of these make delightful gifts when dressed in pretty embroidered covers or labels, complete with appropriate motifs.

JAR COVERS AND LABELS

YOU WILL NEED

For each lacy jar cover, measuring approximately 12cm (4³/₄in), excluding the lace trim:

15cm (6in) square of 14-count Aida fabric in either oatmeal or cream
Stranded embroidery cotton in the colours given in the appropriate panel
No24 tapestry needle
75cm (30in) of lace trim, 2cm (³/₄in) deep, with evenly-spaced holes along one edge, for the ribbon
1m (1yd) of narrow ribbon, to match one of the embroidery colours
Sewing thread to match the fabric

For each label, measuring 9.7cm × 6cm (3⁷/₈in × 2³/₈in):

12.5cm × 9cm (5in × 3¹/₂in) of 14-count, dark green ('Bayleaf') Aida fabric
Stranded embroidery cotton in the colours given in the appropriate panel
No24 tapestry needle
60cm (24in) of narrow ribbon, to match one of the embroidery colours
12.5cm × 9cm (5in × 3¹/₂in) of iron-on fabric stiffener (optional)

•

THE EMBROIDERY

For either a lacy jar cover or a label, first prepare the fabric, marking the centre with vertical and horizontal lines of basting stitches in a light-coloured thread (see page 4), then mount the fabric in a small hoop (see page 5). It is not always necessary to start in the centre of such a small piece of embroidery, but it is important to ensure that the centre stitch of the chart will be at the centre of your fabric.

For a jar cover, use two strands of embroidery cotton in the needle for cross stitches and to backstitch the mint stems, then use just one strand for all other backstitches.

For the bottle labels, use two strands of thread in the needle for all cross stitches, and then one strand for the backstitches.

LACY JAR COVER

For each cover, leaving the basting stitches in place as guidelines, lightly draw a circle, 12cm (4³/₄in) in diameter, on the right side of the fabric, using a pencil and keeping the embroidery centred. Either machine zigzag around the circle and then cut it out, or cut it out and oversew the edges by hand to prevent fraying. Remove basting stitches.

Neatly join the short edges of the lace trim, then run a gathering thread around the edge and gather it to fit the fabric circle. Stitch the lace around the fabric, by hand or machine, with the lace overlapping the fabric by about 5mm (scant ¹/₄in).

Starting at a point opposite to the join in the lace, thread the ribbon through the holes in the lace (you may find it easiest to do this with a large tapestry needle). To use the cover, tie the ribbon ends into a bow, gathering the cover around the top of the jar.

LABEL

Make a small paper pattern/template, and draw the shape on the back of your embroidered fabric, keeping the embroidery centred. Cut out, adding a 6mm (¹/₄in) seam allowance all round.

If you are using stiffener, draw the same outline on your fabric stiffener; cut out along the outline, then iron the stiffener to the back of the embroidery.

Oversew the edges of the embroidery fabric if necessary, then turn in the seam allowance all around, making neat corners, and hem. Cut the ribbon in half, and stitch a length to each side of the label.

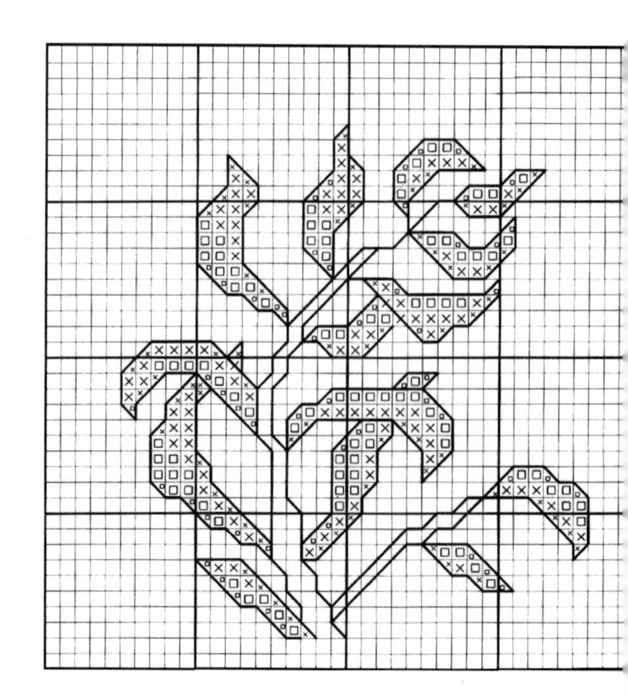

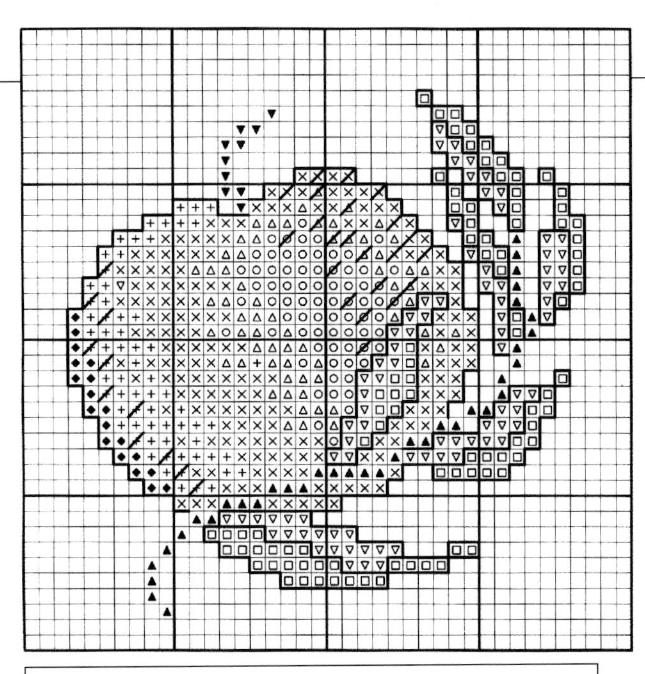

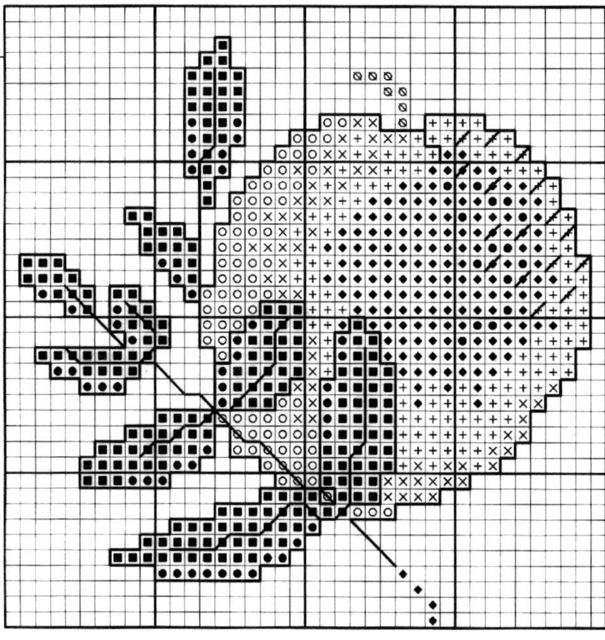

APPLE AND SAGE ▲		DMC	ANCHOR	MADEIRA
◆	Light mint green	472	278	1414
○	Burnt orange	922	1003	0311
△	Orange	721	324	0309
X	Gold	741	304	0201
+	Pale yellow	3078	292	0111
▲	Dark sage green	500	879	1705
□	Medium sage green	501	877	1704
▽	Light sage green	502	875	1703
▼	Ochre	729	890	2203

Note: backstitch around the apple in burnt orange and around the leaves in dark sage green, using one strand of thread in the needle.

APPLE AND MINT ▲		DMC	ANCHOR	MADEIRA
◆	Light mint green	472	278	1414
●	Medium mint green	471	266	1409
■	Dark mint green	3345	263	1507
○	Burnt orange	922	1003	0311
X	Gold	741	304	0201
+	Pale yellow	3078	292	0111
⦸	Light ochre	676	891	2012

Note: backstitch around the apple in burnt orange and around the leaves in medium mint green, using one strand of thread in the needle.

ROSEMARY ▼		DMC	ANCHOR	MADEIRA
●	Green	3345	263	1507
X	Light mint green	472	278	1414
◆	Lavender	793	176	0902
◇	Light lavender	341	117	0901

Note: backstitch in light mint green, using one strand of thread in the needle.

LABEL TEMPLATE
FULL SIZE

TARRAGON ◀		DMC	ANCHOR	MADEIRA
□	Olive	471	266	1409
X	Light mint green	472	278	1414

Note: backstitch in light mint green, using one strand of thread in the needle.

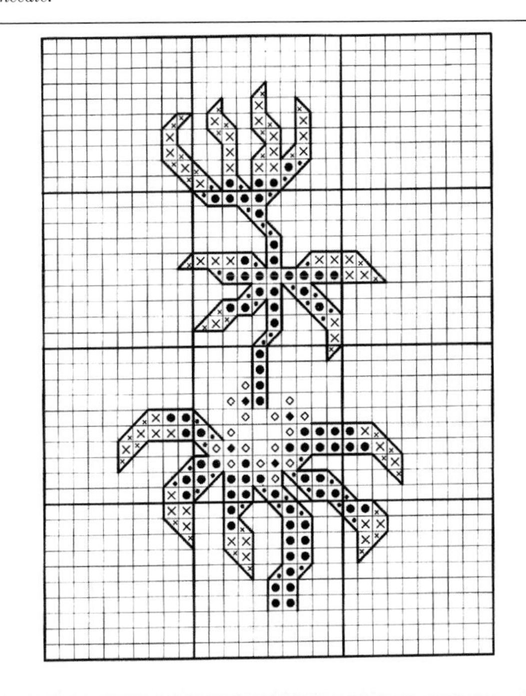

ACKNOWLEDGEMENTS

Thanks are due to Mike, Daniel and Liam for their patience. To Adele Bates, Julie and Richard Morgan, and Elaine Dale, thank you for your help along the way.

SUPPLIERS

The following companies have supplied materials used in the projects in this book:
Rose and Hubble Ltd (embroidery fabrics),
Fabric Flair (other fabrics), and DMC Creative World Ltd.
Framecraft Miniatures, listed below, is a mail order company that is a useful source of supply for cross stitch items, including blank embroidery cards, picture frames and linens.

Rose and Hubble Ltd
Sandringham Way
Withymoor Village
Brierley Hill
West Midlands DY5 3JR
Telephone: 01384 7789

FRAMECRAFT
Fabric Flair Ltd
The Old Brewery
The Close
Warminster
Wiltshire BA12 9AL
Telephone: 01985 214466

Framecraft Miniatures Limited
372/376 Summer Lane
Hockley
Birmingham, B19 3QA
England
Telephone: 0121 359 4442

Addresses for Framecraft stockists worldwide
Ireland Needlecraft Pty Ltd
2-4 Keppel Drive
Hallam, Victoria 3803
Australia

Danish Art Needlework
PO Box 442, Lethbridge
Alberta T1J 3Z1
Canada

Sanyei Imports
PO Box 5, Hashima Shi
Gifu 501-62
Japan

The Embroidery Shop
286 Queen Street
Masterton
New Zealand

Anne Brinkley Designs Inc.
246 Walnut Street
Newton
Mass. 02160
USA

S A Threads and Cottons Ltd.
43 Somerset Road
Cape Town
South Africa

For information on your nearest stockist of embroidery cotton, contact the following:

DMC
(also distributors of Zweigart fabrics)
UK
DMC Creative World Limited
62 Pullman Road, Wigston
Leicester, LE8 2DY
Telephone: 0116 2811040

USA
The DMC Corporation
Port Kearney Bld.
10 South Kearney
N.J. 07032-0650
Telephone: 201 589 0606

AUSTRALIA
DMC Needlecraft Pty
P.O. Box 317
Earlswood 2206
NSW 2204
Telephone: 02599 3088

COATS AND ANCHOR
Coats Paton Crafts
McMullen Road
Darlington
Co. Durham DL1 1YQ
Telephone: 01325 381010

USA
Coats & Clark
P.O. Box 27067
Dept CO1
Greenville SC 29616
Telephone: 803 234 0103

AUSTRALIA
Coats Patons Crafts
Thistle Street
Launceston
Tasmania 7250
Telephone: 00344 4222

MADEIRA

UK
Madeira Threads (UK) Limited
Thirsk Industrial Park
York Road, Thirsk
N. Yorkshire, YO7 3BX
Telephone: 01845 524880

USA
Madeira Marketing Limited
600 East 9th Street
Michigan City
IN 46360
Telephone: 219 873 1000

AUSTRALIA
Penguin Threads Pty Limited
25-27 Izett Street
Prahran
Victoria 3181
Telephone: 03529 4400